THE ROMAN VILLA AT BRADFORD ON AVON

The Investigations of 2002

Mark Corney

EX LIBRIS PRESS

Published in 2003 by
Ex Libris Press
1 The Shambles
Bradford on Avon
Wiltshire
BA15 1JS

www.ex-librisbooks.co.uk

Origination by Ex Libris Press

Printed by Cromwell Press
Trowbridge

ISBN 1 903341 17 5

INTRODUCTION

D uring July and August 2002, a three-week season of archaeological fieldwork was undertaken on and around the sports field of St Laurence School, Bradford on Avon, by students and specialists from the Universities of Bristol and Cardiff. This was designed to be a reconnaissance exercise pending the formulation of a long-term project into the Romano-British landscape of the Bradford on Avon area. The results were beyond the team's expectations and fired the imagination and support of many people in the Bradford area. The following is an account of the background to the 2002 excavation and the results of the first season.

All excavations and field projects involve a great many individuals with a wide range of expertise. The work at St Laurence is no exception and it is a pleasure to acknowledge the contributions of the following: Dr Peter Guest, University of Cardiff, co-director of the 2002 season; trench supervisors Nick Beaudry, Bill Moffatt, Matt Symonds; finds and post–excavation officer Jane Bircher; all the students from Bristol and Cardiff who worked (and played) so hard to ensure a successful season. The work would not have been possible without the consent, support and encouragement of the Headmaster and Governors of St Laurence School. The Headmaster, Nick Sorensen, took a close interest in all aspects of the work and gave the team much encouragement. Sophie Hawke, an

3

administrator at the School, gave invaluable assistance as liaison officer between the School and the excavation team. We owe a great deal to the School for tolerating us through part of the term and allowing us use of many facilities. Finally, a warm vote of thanks is due to so many of the people of Bradford on Avon who showed such interest and enthusiasm for the work. It is a particular pleasure to thank 'Sparky' for his practical support (and ice-cream), Martin Valatin who first drew my attention to the site and Roger Jones of Ex Libris Press for inviting me to produce this brief account of the work.

BRADFORD BEFORE THE ROMAN CONQUEST

The early prehistory of the Bradford area is poorly understood, comprising mainly of scatters of worked flint tools and a few possible burial mounds of the Bronze Age. It is only at the beginning of the Iron Age, approximately 700-600BC, that we have firm evidence for settlement. At Budbury, on the plateau edge overlooking the present town, a large enclosed settlement was established. Regrettably, much of this important site was destroyed without record. A rescue excavation in the late 1960's by Dr Geoffrey Wainwright provided an outline sequence demonstrating intermittent use of the site from the early Iron Age (c600BC) until the end of the Roman period. The presence of this major prehistoric settlement may provide a clue as to why the Roman villa developed on the plateau only 500 metres away.

The distribution of pre-Roman coins suggests that Bradford lay within the area of an Iron Age tribe known as the 'Dobunni', a large confederation whose territory extended from the northern edge of Mendip, across the Cotswolds, and into Herefordshire and Worcestershire. The Dobunni had been in receipt of luxury goods from the Roman world for fifty or more years before the Roman conquest of AD43. Wine jars (*amphorae*) from central Italy and high quality pottery from Gaul (modern France) have been found at a number of sites within Dobunnic territory and it possible that the tribe had established diplomatic relations with Rome. The main centres of the Dobunni were in the Cirencester region, with large settlements at Bagendon (north of Cirencester), Salmonsbury (near Bourton on the Water) and possibly Minchinhampton near Stroud. Other centres probably await discovery and one may have existed in the Bath region.

ROMANS IN THE
BRADFORD AREA (Fig.1)

B radford on Avon is situated in an area of fertile land with good natural communications by land and river. Such a location will have been extensively settled and cultivated long before the Roman conquest. Air photographs have revealed extensive prehistoric fields and tracks between the town and Corsham. To the west of Bradford and south of the modern Bath road (A363), the earthwork remains of similar fields are still visible as subtle surface features.

All of the archaeological evidence points to this landscape experiencing a peaceful transition to Roman rule. Unlike other parts of the southwest, such as Dorset, there is no hint of the Roman army having to attack and subdue hostile populations. The nearest Roman forts to Bradford on Avon are at Bath, Cirencester and Mildenhall near Marlborough. Established soon after the invasion of AD43, these bases will have been primarily concerned with local policing, administration and military supply. All were abandoned by the early to mid 70's AD and a formally structured local civilian administration was established at Cirencester, supplemented by small market towns and roadside settlements such as Nettleton (near Castle Coombe) and Camerton (near Radstock).

Whilst based in the region, the Roman military will have been instrumental in establishing the core infrastructure for the incoming civil administration. This will have included the construction of the main road network, including the Fosse Way, the surveying and laying-out of urban centres such as Bath and Cirencester, and the stimulation of local agrarian and industrial production.

The archaeology of the first hundred years after AD43 in the Bradford area is limited. There are very few sites of this period that have been investigated in sufficient detail and it is anticipated that the St Laurence School site will provide valuable evidence as work progresses. Many local villas have produced first and second century material such as pottery, brooches and coins, but few have provided detailed structural information due to later Roman building activity.

The origins and development of villas in the earlier Roman period is still poorly understood. The buildings that we see on most villas in Britain date from the third and fourth centuries AD. It is anticipated that, as investigations continue at St Laurence School, this elusive period may be revealed. There is strong circumstantial evidence that the majority of villas develop on, or adjacent to, later Iron Age settlements. This pattern would suggest that the villas are the homes of Britons, possibly of high status, who become romanised and, as wealth is accrued, begin to re-model their homes in a Roman style. The villa excavated at Atworth, only 5km north of Bradford, produced a great deal of first and second century material, suggesting earlier Roman occupation, although no structures of this date have been identified. At Box, a villa of palatial proportions, earlier material is present and some of the buildings may originate in the second century.

In addition to the villas, other types of settlement are known. Air photography has revealed a number of settlements that may belong to the later prehistoric and early Roman periods. Between Bradford and Corsham an extensive network of fields, tracks and settlements show a continuation of the landscape pattern established in the Iron Age. Some of the settlement sites have produced surface finds of first and second century pottery although none has yet been excavated.

These are mainly small farms, probably representing the homes of extended families that may have been dependent upon the leading families or clans who were to become the villa owners. Several of these sites are known in the Bradford area although none have been excavated. Where known, these farms are set within field systems integrated with tracks giving access to the surrounding fields and linking up to the main Roman road network. A number of such farms are known or suspected to the west and northwest of Bradford on the limestone plateau around Inwood and Warleigh Woods.

Before the discovery of the villa complex at St Laurence School, the evidence of Roman occupation in Bradford was relatively slight but significant. Five stone coffins of later Roman date are known. Four come from the plateau, within 500 metres of the villa site. The same area has also produced stray finds of Roman pottery and coins. A further stone coffin was found at the foot of the hill below Budbury, near Barton Orchard, some time before 1907. The presence of stone coffins indicated that there ought to be a Roman settlement of some substance in the area. Such items would have been expensive and are generally held to indicate persons of some considerable local status. Two of these coffins, one for an adult and one for a child can be seen outside the entrance to the main administrative building at St Laurence School (Plate 1). The excavations at Budbury hillfort also produced quantities of later Roman pottery and coins, and numerous coins ranging from second to fourth century date have been found in the Budbury area generally. The first significant hint of a major building complex came in 1976 when part of a bath-house was discovered and partially excavated. This was located at one corner of the St Laurence School playing field, adjacent to Bear Close. It was a well-built structure and displayed the standard Roman bathing arrangement of hot (*caldarium*), warm (*tepidarium*) and cold (*frigidarium*) rooms. The building was dated to the later third century AD and continued in use until the late fourth or early fifth century AD. It produced a number of fine architectural fragments and large quantities of painted wall-plaster. This structure is now known to have been located in one wing of the main villa complex. The limited excavation was not able to define the full extent of the range. Thus was the state of knowledge until the early summer of 1999.

THE DISCOVERY AND INITIAL INVESTIGATION OF THE VILLA COMPLEX

S taff and pupils at St Laurence School had long been aware of strange marks appearing on the school playing field during long hot spells in the summer. It was widely believed that these marks showed the outline of a buried building although no report was made. It was only in the summer of 1999 that the marks were recorded by Bradford architect, Martin Valatin, who passed the information on to the Wiltshire County Archaeologist, Mr Roy Canham. An aerial photographic sortie was arranged through English Heritage and the resulting photographs, coupled with Mr Valatin's plan, revealed the unmistakable plan of a Roman villa with at least 15 rooms in the main range and further wings extending beyond the southern boundary of the playing field. The main building measures 38 metres (118 feet) by 18 metres (56 feet). Following this confirmation of a villa building, students from the University of Bristol undertook a geophysical survey of the area under the direction of Dr Richard Tabor and the author (Plate 2). This added further detail to data derived from the air and ground survey, and, much to the surprise of all involved, revealed a second house of identical size and plan. This was on the same alignment as the first building discovered and set 30 metres (over 90 feet) to the west of it (Fig. 2).

The plan revealed by the non-invasive methods outlined is without parallel in Roman Britain. Villa plans can be categorised according to form and layout such as 'courtyard' and 'winged corridor'. The two main houses at Bradford belong to the latter type, a form well known in western Britain. Although 'double houses' are known they are usually paired integral structures linked by a corridor or, as at Halstock in Dorset, by a probable tower over an entrance passage between the two houses.

The eastern house at St Laurence has two ranges projecting to the south, the western arm of which housed the bath-suite excavated in 1976. The full extent of the ranges is unknown as they extend under a modern housing estate, although the available evidence suggests that they are at least 60 metres (188 feet) in length. The western house does not appear to have similar ranges, although the geophysics suggests that features are present to the south of the house. These may be part of an earlier building or components of a formal garden.

In addition to the extensive building remains, the geophysical survey also located a number of ditches. These share a different alignment to the villa remains and may be part of a later prehistoric or early Roman landscape (Fig. 3).

During the course of the survey work it was also noticed that the drystone walls marking the western boundary of the school property contain a high proportion of roughly dressed and squared stone blocks. An initial visual inspection of the walls suggests that these are most frequent close to the villa site. There is a very strong possibility that these blocks are derived from the superstructure of

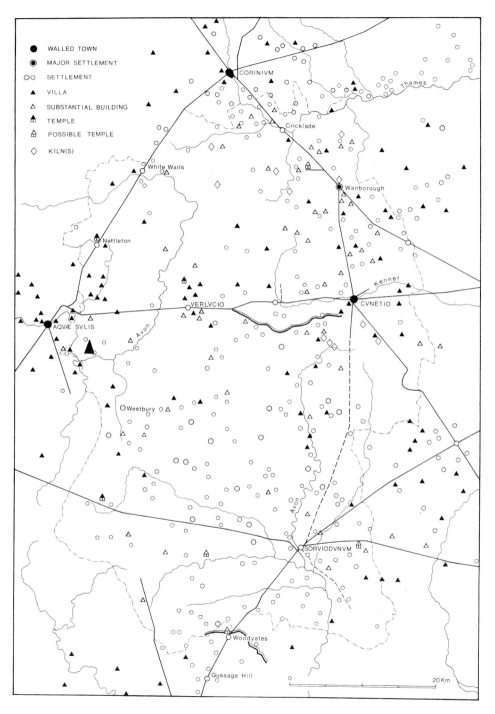

Figure 1. Roman Wiltshire, the Bradford villa is indicated by the large triangle

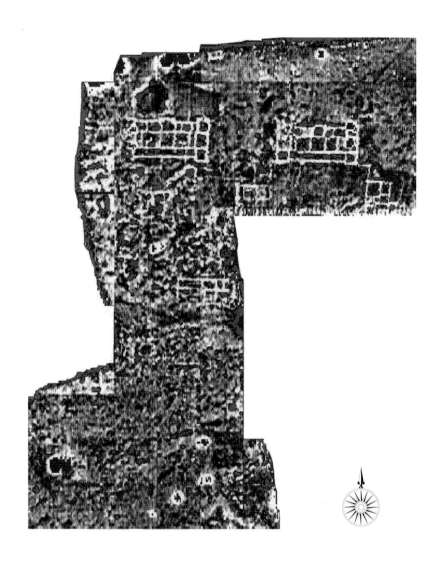

Figure 2. The geophysical survey

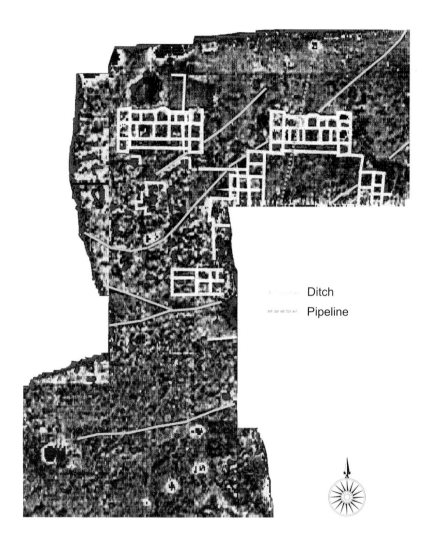

Ditch

Pipeline

Figure 3. Geophysical survey: interpretation. The bold white lines represent the buried walls

Plate 1: Roman stone coffin at St Laurence School

Plate 2: The geophysical survey showing magnetometer in use

Above – Plate 3: Stone stile to the west of the villa site. The shape and form of the block suggests that it is a piece of re-used masonry from the villa buildings, possibly a door jamb

Left: Plate 4: Stone door jambs at the Roman villa of Great Witcombe, near Gloucester

Plate 5: Trench 1. General view looking west

Plate 6: Trench 1. Late Roman decapitated burial as excavated. The head has been carefully placed between the lower legs

Plate 7: Trench 2. The hypocaust

Plate 8: Pre-villa plough marks

Above – Plate 9: Trench 3. The foundations of the apsidal room as excavated

Right – Plate 10: Trench 3. Junction of the two-phase walling

Plate 11: Trench 4. Collapsed wall and roof resting on the mosaic floor

Plate 13: Detail of the mosaic showing the Cantharus *and flanking dolphins*

Plate 12: Trench 4. The mosaic fully excavated

Plate 14: Detail of the mosaic showing stylised foliage motif

Plate 15: Cut through the mosaic floor. A post-Roman grave?

Plate 16: Trench 4. Roof and wall debris overlying a mortar floor

Plate 17: Earthwork survey to the west of the villa

the villa. Approximately 400 metres (1200 feet) to the west of the villa, a stile set into a drystone wall was discovered to be a single, large dressed monolith 2 metres (6 feet) in length (Plate 3). This is without doubt a re-used item of Roman stonework, being identical in shape and form to surviving doorjambs still to be seen at the Roman villa of Great Witcombe near Gloucester (Plate 4). A more detailed survey of the drystone walling adjacent to St Laurence School will no doubt reveal further components of the villa buildings.

The initial investigation of the complex had demonstrated the presence of a major Roman complex with great potential for further study employing a wide range of modern archaeological techniques.

THE INVESTIGATIONS OF 2002

In July 2002, the Universities of Bristol and Cardiff undertook a preliminary series of investigations as a collaborative project. This had limited aims and was designed to provide information for the formulation of long-term research strategy to investigate the villa and its landscape. The objectives were:

1 Through excavation, to establish an outline chronology for the two winged corridor buildings and to test the state of preservation and survival of archaeological deposits.

2 To undertake preliminary landscape analysis using earthwork survey, geophysical survey, air photographic interpretation and recording of stonework in field walls.

Excavation

Excavation was confined to four small areas; one on the eastern house, two over the western house and a short trench south of the western house.

The first trench, 1, was sited to the south of the western building to check for further possible structures. The geophysical survey was unclear in this area due to the close proximity of a chain-link fence. Measuring 2 metres by 10 metres, trench 1 revealed a very shallow

14

depth of plough soil resting directly onto limestone bedrock (Plate 5). At the western end, there was the outline of a cut into the bedrock, with pick marks clearly visible and backfilled with large limestone slabs and dark brown soil. Removal of this fill soon began to reveal human bones and it was realised that we had encountered a grave. Small pieces of Roman pottery from the fill made it clear that this was an ancient burial. Work had to be suspended whilst the Wiltshire County Coroner was informed and a licence to exhume the remains was sought from the Home Office. Having completed the legal requirements, excavation of the grave resumed. Aligned northwest-southeast with the feet towards the southeast, the burial proved to be an example of an unusual late Roman to early post-Roman rite. There were no grave goods apart from a number of hobnails at the feet, suggesting burial with stout shoes or sandals. The head had been removed and placed between the legs (Plate 6). The edge of a second grave on the same alignment was noted running beyond the limit of the trench but not investigated.

This discovery was unexpected. The proximity of this probable cemetery to the villa buildings suggests that it is very late Roman or, most likely, early post Roman in date. Cemeteries associated with villas during their main period of occupation tend to occur at some distance from the domestic buildings. The burials discovered in 2002 are only 35m (just over 100 feet) south of the western villa house where gardens may reasonably be expected.

Although the rite of post-mortem decapitation is relatively unusual, other examples are known from a number of sites in western Britain. The reason for this somewhat disturbing practice is uncertain. Execution seems unlikely as much of the pathological evidence from other examples points to the head being removed by cutting into the neck from the front. Many believe that the rite may reflect a fear of the deceased and by removing the head, the spirit is prevented from returning to haunt the living.

The second area of excavation was placed over the south corner of the western villa house. Based on comparisons with other villas of similar plan, it was anticipated that this would be a substantial part of the structure and would have probably supported a tower of two or even three storeys. The top of the Roman walling began to appear at a depth of approximately 40-50 centimetres (14 -18 inches). The walls were almost 1 metre (over 3 feet) thick, constructed of squared limestone blocks with up to two courses of mortared masonry surviving above the level of the natural bedrock. Excavation of the room interior soon revealed a mass of fragmented stone slabs and the tops of stone piers. It rapidly became apparent that we had encountered the remains of a heated room or *hypocaust* system (Plate 7). The slabs had originally been placed over the stone piers (or *pilae*) to support the original floor surface, no trace of which survived. As excavation proceeded it was discovered that part of this room had been damaged during the eighteenth century by a large, irregular shaped pit, and several of the stone *pilae* removed. The pit was dated by an assemblage of mid to late eighteenth century pottery and clay pipe fragments. Given the date of this intrusion it is surprising that no record survives of this activity. By this date, 'Antiquarianism' is a popular pursuit for gentlemen and many Roman discoveries were being made and reported upon over much of England.

Excavation of the *hypocaust* will be completed in summer 2003 and the next room to the north, where the furnace was located, will be examined. The fill of the hypocaust has already produced an important body of dating evidence relating to the final phases of activity in this building. Initial assessment of the finds suggests that the *hypocaust* ceased to function at the end of the fourth or early fifth century AD. The floor was partially removed and the cavity used as a rubbish dump for domestic debris including a large deposit of animal bone. Pottery and glass, some of the latter possibly from the Rhineland, suggests that there was still activity and occupation in the immediate vicinity in the early fifth century or later.

To the west and south of this room, in areas that would have been outside the house, the limestone bedrock was found to be covered in shallow, parallel grooves. These were on two alignments, at 90° to each other and were clearly earlier than the Roman building. It was quickly realised that they were ancient plough-marks where the tip of a primitive type of plough, known as an ard, had cut into the limestone (Plate 8). This is important evidence for pre-villa activity. Although no datable objects were associated with the marks, comparison with similar marks found on the Wessex chalk suggests that they are later prehistoric. This is the first discovery of this type on the Wiltshire limestone.

A further part of this building was examined in trench 3. Sited over what was thought to be the main room on the ground floor, it was centrally located on the north side of the building and the geophysics suggested that it featured a north-projecting apse. Confirmation of the plan was soon achieved, as the remains were only 30-35 centimetres (12-14 inches) below the surface. Only the lowest course of the foundations for the apsidal room survived (Plate 9). These comprised unmortared blocks with pitched-stone infilling. The south wall of the room was better preserved and was of similar construction to the room excavated in trench 2. The difference in walling construction suggested at least two phases of building with the apsidal room being a later addition (Plate 10). No floor levels survived within the apsidal room. Despite the poor state of preservation, the trench provided valuable dating evidence for the two phases of construction.

The southern wall of the apsidal room appears to have originally formed the north wall of a simple, rectangular building. This may well be the original villa house. Initial study of pottery associated with construction levels would indicate a date between cAD160 and AD230. This fits well with other villas in western Britain and marks a period of growing prosperity in the Romano-British countryside. The addition of the apsidal room did not occur before cAD270/80 and may be as late as cAD300+. This later date again fits well with other sites in the region, the late third to mid fourth century marking the climax of villa building and structural aggrandisement. The lack of any surviving superstructure or floor levels associated with the apsidal room makes detailed analysis difficult and the room and adjacent rooms to the east and west may have never been completed.

Below the level of the apsidal room, outcrops of limestone bedrock featured plough-marks identical to those discovered in trench 2.

The fourth and final trench was located over the apsidal room in the eastern villa house. This was selected to allow direct comparison with its counterpart in the western house. The soil cover here proved to be very shallow due to grading of the playing field in the 1970's. Removal of the turf immediately exposed a layer of limestone rubble and the tops of walling (Plate 11). The rubble was clearly collapsed walling from the villa superstructure and in turn overlay a spread of pennant sandstone roof tiles. After the careful planning of these deposits, they were removed revealing the room plan and a very well-preserved mosaic floor. What appeared to be an rounded apsidal room on the geophysics in fact proved upon excavation to be a semi-hexagonal apse. Within this room, which measured 4.5 x 5.2 metres (approximately 14 x 16 feet) was a mosaic floor (Plate 12). In the apse, the motif comprised a *cantharus* (a two-handled vase) flanked by dolphins (Plate 13). The main panel featured a central rosette and knot motif with the four corners filled with stylised foliage (Plate 14). The style, quality and condition of the mosaic make it one of the finest to have been discovered in Wiltshire for over 30 years. The mosaic was examined and recorded by the leading British authority on the topic, Dr David Neal. Dr Neal dates the floor to cAD350-360 and believes it was laid by craftsmen from Cirencester. The Cirencester (or *Corinian* – after the Roman name for Cirencester, *Corinium*) School of mosaicists was the most accomplished in late Roman Britain, being responsible for some of the finest mosaics in the province. The floor exposed is only part of a larger one. The border of the second component was seen on the southern edge of the trench but given constraints on time and resources, was not excavated.

This is a major discovery. It is clear, using comparisons with other sites, that the eastern house had an imposing bi-partite room set on the line of central access to the house. Anyone entering the house would have come through a porch, into a corridor and then looked into the bi-partite room with the semi-hexagonal apse at the far end. It is here that the owner would have waited to greet guests or important visitors and was the formal and public heart of the house.

One part of the mosaic floor had been damaged before the collapse of the roof and walls. An irregular shaped hole in the floor, aligned east-west and measuring approximately 1 x 2 metres (3 x 6 feet), abutted the west wall of the room (Plate 15). This has yet to be examined. In other villas in western Britain, post-Roman burials, generally undated, have been recorded cutting through mosaic floors. One theory is that these may be early post-Roman Christian burials and mark a conversion of one or more rooms into a 'house church'. Whether this should be the case at St Laurence will have to await further excavation. Whatever the feature may turn out to be, it is of considerable importance as any datable material within it may help to ascertain when the villa finally fell into ruin.

Examination of a small area on the outside of the semi-hexagonal apse wall was excavated to define the character of the foundations. This established that the semi-hexagonal apse was part of a secondary phase and had replaced a rounded apse. No closely datable material was recovered from this area and the precise chronology of the development of the eastern house will have to await further investigation.

To the east of the mosaic part of a further room was exposed. This was also covered by collapsed debris sealing a floor of white mortar and containing pottery of late fourth century AD date (Plate 16).

Non-intrusive survey

One of great attractions of the site is the accessibility of the surrounding landscape for study. Areas to the north and west of the villa complex display subtle surface undulations marking former banks, ditches and other features that probably relate to the villa landscape.

An earthwork survey was undertaken in a small field immediately to the west of the villa complex (Plate 17). This recorded a number of linear features on a common alignment with probable ditches located by geophysical survey in the school playing field (Fig. 5). Some of these earthworks are without doubt the remains of field boundaries that may even pre-date the construction of the villa. Others have the appearance of low platforms and indicate the presence of ancillary structures. A large villa-based estate will have required a great many agricultural buildings for storage and processing. Such an estate will also have been labour intensive and a settlement, or settlements, for estate workers must exist nearby.

Field reconnaissance elsewhere in the immediate area has identified other targets for non-intrusive survey. These are to be recorded in detail over the coming seasons.

The houses and gardens surrounding the villa site are another potentially important source of information for mapping the full extent of the building complex. Plans are being made for pupils from St Laurence School to assist in a survey asking all residents to retain any finds from their gardens. These can be collected, examined and the data used to define further areas of activity. This will be particularly important in the area south of the school playing field where the geophysical survey and information already received from some residents indicates the presence of further buildings.

Air photography is another important component in mapping and understanding the Romano-British landscape. Preliminary examination of air photographs held by English Heritage has identified further elements of field-systems, trackways and possible settlements. The accurate mapping of these will continue and provide further targets for non-intrusive survey methods.

IN CONCLUSION

The combination of excavation and non-intrusive survey has established the presence of a major Romano-British villa complex and its landscape in the vicinity of St Laurence School. Although the investigations are at an early stage, we can already make some general comments on the site sequence.

The earliest Roman building on the site so far identified is the core of the western villa house. This can be dated to a period between cAD160-AD230. This house was enlarged towards the end of the third century AD or the early fourth century AD. The eastern house was certainly in existence by the end of the third century AD and the bath-house excavated in 1976 is part of this complex and contemporary with it. During the middle of the fourth century AD the eastern house underwent alterations with a rounded apse principle room being replaced by one with a semi-hexagonal apse and a high quality mosaic floor.

Both houses continued to be used into the fifth century AD. We cannot yet be certain how long into the fifth century a recognisable Romanised style of living continued. In the western villa house a hypocaust was dismantled and the cavity re-used for the disposal of rubbish. Although this effectively ends the original use of this room, the presence of domestic debris clearly shows that occupation continued nearby and it is possible that a reduced size house was now being occupied. A similar pattern has recently been recorded at the villa at Frocester Court, near Stroud.

In the eastern house occupation in the central range continued for an unknown length of time. At some point, an east-west large cut was made through the mosaic floor. At the time this was made the building was still standing and retained its roof, the feature being sealed by roof and wall collapse.

At the end of the fourth century or during the earlier fifth century AD a cemetery was established a short distance to the south of the western villa house.

The origins of the villa complex are still obscure. In all excavated areas significant quantities of late Iron Age and earlier Roman pottery were found. This would suggest that an earlier phase must exist close by. This has still to be located, although a cluster of ditches on the geophysical survey south of the western villa house may belong to this phase. If an earlier complex can be confirmed through further fieldwork, then it is possible that the later Roman villa complex was the ultimate successor to Budbury hillfort, only 500 metres (1500 feet) to the south east.

The excavations have already demonstrated, through the recognition of plough-marks, that at least part of the villa area had been under cultivation before construction of the villa. Study of earthworks and air photographs has revealed an extensive relict landscape in the area around St Laurence School. Further work will be required to elucidate the chronology and sequence.

As to who lived in the villa, we can only speculate at this stage. It is highly probable that the majority of villa owning families were of British origin, possibly the descendants of late tribal Iron Age aristocrats. At some sites we can see hints of this, such as the villa at

Piddington in Northamptonshire. Here, bricks and tiles stamped with the family name suggest that their forebears received Roman citizenship at the time of the conquest under the emperor Claudius.

Despite the fact that the villa remains are now no more than foundations and a few courses of walling, we can speculate on the original appearance. In recent years a number of sites have been excavated where collapsed walls have been discovered. At Meonstoke in Hampshire and Redlands Farm, Northamptonshire the evidence demonstrated two-storeyed villa structures. We can also cite contemporary Roman depictions on wall-paintings and mosaics showing substantial structures of two or more storeys. The 'winged-corridor' plan of the St Laurence villas could be reconstructed as having two storeys with the wings rising to three-storeyed towers. Such a complex would have been a dominant feature in the landscape and visible from a great distance.

The ultimate fate of the villa buildings has still to be investigated. The ruins may have been visible for some considerable period before finally being robbed for building stone. It is interesting to note that in the late eighteenth century the field within which the villa lay was called 'Church Ground' – a name sometimes associated with a folk memory of a substantial structure. It is possible that the land holdings of the estate survived even longer. One of the future questions for the project will be to examine the estate granted to St Aldhelm in 705 and attempt to date the boundary and test for a pre-Anglo-Saxon origin. This is just one of the many questions we will attempt to answer.

Over the next two years further fieldwork will be undertaken and without a doubt will lead to new discoveries – and reassessments of the work undertaken to date.